IMAGES
of Ireland

NORTH BELFAST

An aerial view of North Belfast in 1927. The Antrim Road is on the right, with the Cavehill Road snaking northwards past the lower and upper ponds of the Waterworks.

IMAGES
of Ireland
NORTH BELFAST

Compiled by
Peggy Weir
With the assistance of
Margaret Cartwright and Daphne McClements

GILL & MACMILLAN

Published in Ireland by
Gill & Macmillan Ltd
Goldenbridge, Dublin 8
with associated companies throughout the world
Copyright © North Belfast Historical Society, 1999, 2000

ISBN 0 7171 2917 9

Typesetting and origination by
Tempus Publishing Limited
Printed in Great Britain by
Midway Clark Printing, Wiltshire

Also published in the *Images of Ireland* series:
Banbridge (Angela Dillon)
Dungannon (Felix Hagan)
East Belfast (Keith Haines)
Enniscorthy (Dan Walsh)
South Belfast (George E. Templeton and Norman Weatherall)
Tralee (Michael Diggin)

Belfast Castle was built by Lord Donegall in 1872 in the Deer Park. The Chapel of the Resurrection was later built for the private use of the Shaftesbury family. The slopes of the Cave Hill were originally used as farm land but from the 1880s trees were planted, producing the now familiar woodland setting for the buildings.

Contents

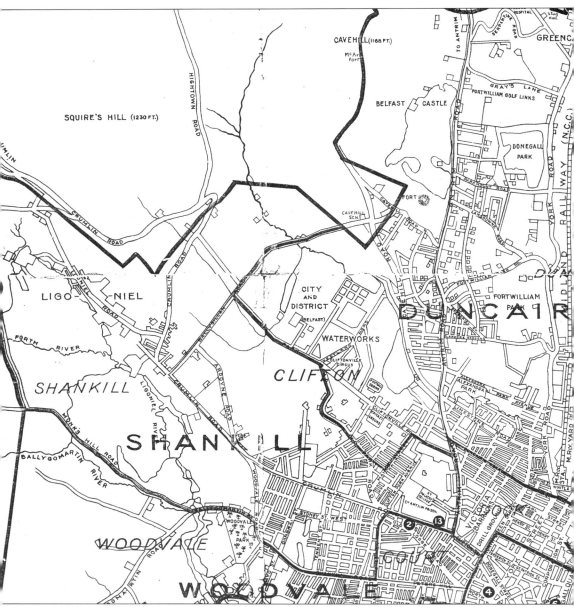

Detail from a street map of North Belfast, 1918.

Introduction

In the times following the last Ice Age much of what is now North Belfast was under water. Evidence of that high tidal period is visible in the ridge along which North Queen Street now runs and in the little steep hills within Grove Park and Fortwilliam.

In its early industrial development Belfast moved northwards from High Street. As recently as the 1830s the northern limit of the growing town was the line of Frederick Street. Beyond that were the large estates of prominent wealthy merchants and bankers. The names of those estates are retained by, for example, Grove, Castleton, Mount Collyer and Mount Vernon. Smaller, reasonably wealthy homes were to be found at Willowbank, Marsden, Old Lodge, Vicinage, Wheatfield, etc. For the richer homes between the present Antrim and Shore Roads the view was idyllic; the fronts faced Belfast Lough and the County Down coast with the unspoilt Cave Hill to the rear. The main road to Antrim was then via Shankill and only bridle paths led over and around Cave Hill.

Industrialists, seeking sites for their new enterprises, built their mills on the Crumlin and Shore Roads and at Greencastle and Ligoniel. When the old estates were eventually broken up the area became residential, recreational and educational. Large open spaces were provided by public parks and Fortwilliam Golf Course. The Castle estate was handed over to the Belfast Corporation for the use of its citizens in 1934. The working classes lived near the mill and dock areas and the middle classes dwelt along the Antrim Road and the thoroughfares opening off it. This situation obtained until the new road developments, commenced in the 1960s, resulted in the demolition of the old working-class districts and the movement of population. Many of the open spaces were built over. While population movement continues it can be expected that no changes of major importance in the area can now occur.

The adage 'one photograph is worth a thousand words' holds true. Even the most eloquent speaker finds difficulty in explaining past social conditions without adequate illustrations. This collection of photographs proves that. School or wedding photographs may appear of interest only to those in the picture or their descendants, but for us they show the alterations in the dress, style and the modes of the times. Buildings, streetscapes, transport and places of entertainment are unimaginable without the camera's product. Each illustration tells of an age now long gone but for memories. So it is necessary for groups such as North Belfast Historical Society to collect, collate and preserve these memories. People and buildings have a limited time span so we rely on memory and the camera to preserve evidence of their existence. This collection does just that.

Fred Heatley
President, North Belfast Historical Society

The foundation stone for the Poor House and Infirmary was laid on 1 August 1771 by Arthur, Lord Donegall. By 1774 the Belfast Charitable Society's lovely Georgian building was ready to house the poor of Belfast.

A.C. Williamson's shop at the corner of York Street and Bentinck Street, *c.* 1912. Note the range of goods stocked.

One
Leisure Pursuits

The grounds of Belfast Castle estate, given to the City by the Earl of Shaftesbury in 1934, are still used by walkers.

The Belvedere at Bellevue Gardens before the Zoo was built. The Tea House can be seen in the background.

Father and son enjoy a paddle-boat ride on the Round Pond.

The famous steps at Bellevue Zoological Gardens opened in 1934.

The Floral Hall, Hazelwood, holds fond memories for the dancers of several decades and is now in a sadly dilapidated condition.

Robert Frame and friends take a Sunday stroll in 1904. The track of the Cavehill railway from the quarry provided access to the hill.

The first Scout troop in North Belfast started in 1911, in 'Mr Eakin's hayloft in Ashley Gardens.' Since then there have been many troops connected with churches and schools as well as some independent troops. These are members of the 6th Belfast Scout troop outside Skegoneill Public Elementary School in 1914.

Mulholland School of Dancing, *c*. 1938. Those pictured include Sally Heffernan, Neilly Heffernan, Peggy Marshall, Peggy Wilson and Noel Marshall.

The Johnston brothers entertain with songs round the piano in 1904.

This football team is believed to have been connected with Spamount Congregational church. James Davison, later Revd James R. Davison, appears in the picture with the football.

The Boys' Brigade of Duncairn Presbyterian church, 1912.

Model yachting on the Waterworks Lower Pond, *c.* 1920. Harry Tregannon was the winner of the World Championship in model yachting several times.

The Upper Pond at the Waterworks, *c.* 1920. Rowing boats could be hired at this jetty.

Patricia Mulholland plays for her medal-winning team at a local festival, *c.* 1938.

Pat Boyd's popular dancing class ready to perform, 1949.

Thrills and spills on Buttermilk Loney, New Year 1939. Boys, mainly from St Malachy's College, are enjoying the snow during the Christmas break, including: Rory Casement, Danny McDaniel, Terry Lording, Enda Casement, Brian Moore, Desmond Taylor, Brian McCusker and Bernard McCloskey. The boy with the cigarette is Brian Moore, the celebrated author, and other boys with him here became distinguished members of the medical, legal and architectural professions.

The Jewish Golfing Society at Fortwilliam in 1991. Raymond Maw (Captain) entertains his fellow members.

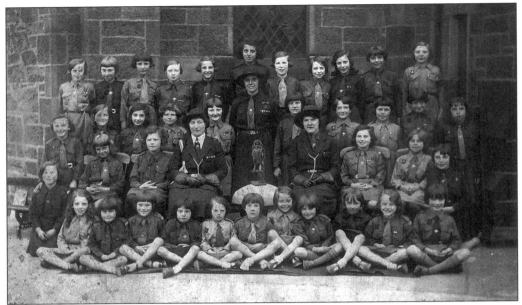

St Enoch's Brownies, *c.* 1930. Brown Owl (Miss Wade) and Tawny Owl (Miss Bell) are surrounded by Brownies.

Jessie and May Thompson are proud Brownies, *c.* 1921.

The members of Cavehill Bowling and Lawn Tennis Club seated in front of the new pavilion. The pavilion, built in 1912 at a cost of £322, was burned down by the Suffragettes in 1914 and rebuilt in 1915.

North Belfast Mission Boys' Club, 1945.

This Guides' Guard of Honour was assembled for the opening of the church of the Resurrection, Cavehill Road, on Easter Sunday 1980.

Two
Industry and Transport

Workers in Craig's Engineering Works, situated in Great Georges Street, in 1890.

Ardoyne Tram Depot in 1953 has a Rebuild tramcar ready to start its journey.

Mr McCune drives his pony and trap on his way to his business.

A Standard Red tramcar at the end of the lines at Greencastle, *c.* 1910. Notice that the boys are barefooted.

The old Beetling Mill in Carr's Glen, *c.* 1950. H. Kirk was the beetler there before 1896 when he moved to Cavehill Bridge Cottages.

Ewart's Spinning Mill, Crumlin Road, in 1953 with a McCreary tramcar en route to the City Hall.

Jessie Moreland (third from the left, front row) with her fellow workers outside Ewart's Mill in around 1908.

A Ford V8 van parked outside Gallaher's tobacco factory in 1936.

Women machinists work under male supervision in the Machine Room, York Street Mill, c. 1910.

Workers in the pipe tobacco room in the export factory of Gallaher's pose for a group photograph in 1936. A picture of King George V hangs on the wall.

Jennymount Mill, North Derby Street, built in 1891 for Phillip Johnston and Company, was one of the many mills which began in the 1890s. The demand for housing created by this expansion gave rise to the vast numbers of 'kitchen houses' erected nearby at the same time.

Walter Mullan attends to a gas lamp on the Crumlin Road, *c.* 1950.

Buttermilk Loney, *c.* 1922. Percy Coaton, jarvey, leads his horse and jaunting car.

A converted horse tram fitted with a snow plough passes the Tram Depot on Shore Road in 1952. The van on the right is an ex-Army Austin 'personal utility' vehicle.

This trolleybus, passing McCune's shop on Shore Road, was the last trolleybus purchased by the Belfast Corporation and is now preserved in England.

Belfast Corporation's first bus route was from City Hall to Cavehill Road. Bus no. 1 sits at the Henderson Avenue terminus on the first day of operation, 4 October 1926.

The old Mater Infirmorum Hospital on the Crumlin Road was built originally as Bedeque House by George Augustus Thompson in around 1865.

This Midland Hotel was built to replace the one destroyed along with the railway station in the air raids of 1941.

Three
Highways and Byways

The cobbled streets of Belfast as they were in around 1887. Little York Street ran from Nile Street to Henry Street. Note the woman in the shop doorway.

Frederick Lane ran off Frederick Street. The woman in the doorway is checking her washing, in October 1887.

All the business premises seen here on York Street in the mid-1960s have since disappeared.

Schoolboys wait to cross Donegall Street, *c.* 1915. The spires of Clifton House and St Patrick's Church can be seen in the background.

Carlisle Circus took its name from Lord Carlisle, Viceroy of Ireland. The new electric trams (introduced in 1905) contrast with the horse-drawn vehicles.

The Gate Lodge of the Waterworks still exists but the Ice House (on the left) has long disappeared. The river runs under the Antrim Road and reappears in Alexandra Park.

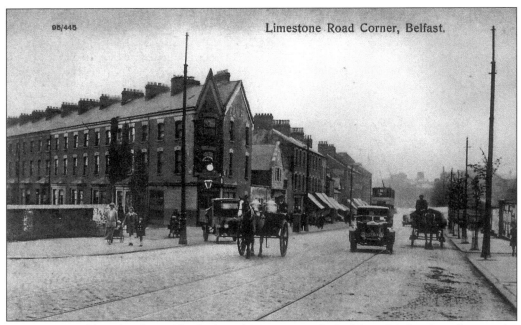

Mrs Henry and her daughters Elizabeth and Margaret with Cathleen McComb walk over the bridge of the Cavehill railway, c. 1925. The milk delivery cart belonged to the Henry family's milkman.

Two boys with bare feet watch the fashionably dressed ladies walk along the Antrim Road, *c.* 1908.

As can be seen in this picture, the part of the Antrim Road beyond the Limestone Road has changed little over the years since 1925.

This springtime scene in around 1913 shows two Standard Red tramcars at Chichester Park.

Robert Frame and friends enjoy a snowball fight at the gates of Fortwilliam Park in 1904.

A Chamberlain tramcar is approaching a stop in front of the Belfast Prison, Crumlin Road. The car on the left is a Vauxhall of the late 1940s.

The twin towers of Holy Cross dominate this part of the Crumlin Road as seen in 1960.

The 'turn of the road' has changed little since this Chamberlain tramcar negotiated it in 1950, heading for Ligoniel village.

Despite the rain these Oldpark Road window cleaners continue their work in around 1947. The houses and shops behind the Moffett tramcar no longer exist.

Cavehill Cottages were lived in for over 100 years until they were demolished in the mid 1960s. Beyond them is the bridge over the old railway track.

Seen through the bridge, the tracks lead up to the Quarry at the foot of the Cave Hill. A group of Scouts prepare for a day's hiking over the Cave Hill in around 1914.

The old railway track, abandoned in the 1890s, can be seen to the left of the Cavehill Road.

Two carts on the old Cavehill Road bring produce from a farm on the slopes of Cave Hill. Belfast Castle can be seen in the background.

These houses on the Cavehill Road, seen across the Waterworks Top Pond, remain much the same today as they were in 1908.

The Ballysillan Road bridged the Carr's Glen river near to Kirkwood's slated and thatched house. This part of the road is still extant but disused since the new road was built.

Wall painting has been popular in Belfast since the turn of the century. The Hedge School picture (above) is from the New Lodge area and the one below from Mount Vernon.

Four
Troubled Times

Waste paper is collected at Mountcollyer School, c. 1940. Connie Watson, Myrtle Patterson, June Ferguson, Violet Millar and Richard McColgan help with the war effort.

Jim Larkin came from Liverpool to Belfast in January 1907 as a National Union of Dock Labourers organizer.

In May 1907 the dockers at the York Dock were on strike in a dispute with the Belfast Steamship Company. Here goods are being delivered to the Fleetwood steamer under police protection.

FLEETWOOD STEAMERS.

Overturned vans at the corner of York Street and Frederick Street after violence associated with the strike, which the carters also joined in. The strike ended in September 1907. A jaunting car stands in the foreground.

During the First World War flax was grown in the grounds of Fortwilliam Golf Club. Here it is being pulled and stooked.

The 14th Battalion of the Royal Irish Rifles marches down the Antrim Road in 1914.

Damage caused by the air raids of 1941 to the International Bar at the corner of Donegall Street and York Street.

The Salisbury Avenue tram depot was badly damaged by an air raid in 1941. Only one of these trams had to be scrapped; the others were repaired.

Precious personal possessions are removed from homes in Sunningdale Park after the air raids of 1941.

American GIs come ashore in Belfast in January 1942.

Cheerful local dockers entertain the newly arrived GIs.

Wartime service personnel are greeted at the door of the synagogue in Annesley Street.

All that remained of the Co-op building after the terrorist bombing on 8 May 1972.

Soldiers sweep the Crumlin Road after the complete destruction of the Wheatfield Bar in 1969.

An armed soldier on patrol in Herbert Street in 1969 stands under a poster appealing for help for children.

Five

The Harbour

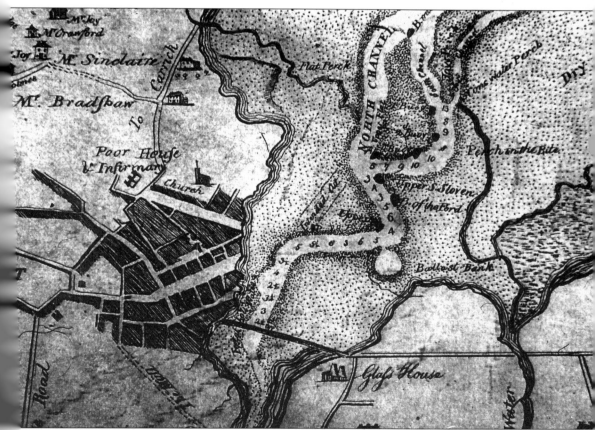

This detail from James Lawson's chart of 1789 shows the town of Belfast and Dargan's Island (now Queen's Island).

The Harbour Office was opened in 1854 and extended in 1895. It was built on the site of Richey's Shipyard.

The opulent 'Public Room' in which special meetings and receptions are held was renovated recently.

The Custom House, opened in 1857, was built on the site of the original Ballast House on Merchant's Quay. The right-hand wing with the additional steps was originally the General Post Office.

The cross-channel steamers at the Donegall Quay, seen from the Queen's Bridge on 18 July 1931.

A flotilla of Royal Navy minesweepers moored at the Pollock Dock, 11 June 1934.

The Prime Minister, Viscount Craigavon, Sir Charles Blackmore CBE and the Harbour Master inspect the sailing ship *Herzogen Cecilie* on 9 July 1935.

The four-masted barque *Herzogen Cecilie* (built in 1902) moored at the Pacific Flour Mills, Pollock Dock. She was wrecked on the south Devon coast in 1936.

In the foreground is Belfast Dry Dock with the Arrol Gantry in the background to the left. The Victoria Channel is on the left and the Herdman Channel to the right.

Rank's Pacific Flour Mill wharf under construction at the Pollock Dock in 1933.

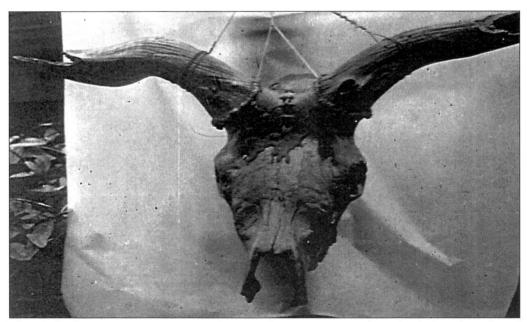

This skull of *Megaceros giganticum* was discovered in January 1932 thirty feet below the red sand during the excavations for the wharf.

Electricity cables being laid across the Herdman Channel, August 1934.

The Headline ship *Ramore Head*, on the left, is making ready to sail. The Herdman Channel is in the background.

This aerial view of the Belfast Harbour area shows the Queen Elizabeth Bridge under construction, *c*. 1964. At that time the cross-channel steamers, moored on the left bank, were still in daily operation.

Six
Schools

Cavehill School was built in 1844 with the parents' own labour using stone from the adjacent quarry transported on the old bogey railway. The Principal, Robert Johnston, is standing in front of the school with his children in around 1880. (See also p. 101.)

Currie Boys' School was situated in Cosgrave Street. The teacher in around 1917 was Miss Gertrude Robinson.

Alexandra School was the site of the present Elim church. This 1927 picture shows the children's clothing styles of the time: note the girl in boots in the front row and the boys with their knitted jerseys and ties.

St Malachy's diocesan seminary was founded in 1833. Later it became a boys' school also and was extended to include a new chapel, classrooms and refectory. A new wing was added in 1882 after the house called Vicinage was demolished.

Between 1910 and 1917 the Lodge in Fortwilliam Park was a school for young ladies run by Miss Elizabeth Rentouil, assisted by her sister Miss Hattie. She believed that 'the strain of preparation for examinations could be injurious to health' and encouraged the playing of croquet and putting and the cultivation of allotments.

St Mark's School was attached to St Mark's church, Ligoniel Road. It was amalgamated with Wolfhill to form Ligoniel Primary School. Here are Standard VII pupils in 1936.

Mr W.R. Patterson sees the children of Skegoneill Primary School safely across Salisbury Avenue, c. 1960.

The pupils of Antrim Road Baptist School ('The Wee Bap') in the playground at the rear of the church with the Principal, Robert Brown, c. 1921.

St Enoch's School, Carlisle Circus, opened in January 1882 with 130 pupils. In 1889 an upper storey was added to the school to provide accomodation for 500 children.

The Holy Family National School was opened in 1914. The girls' school was on the first floor and the boys' school on the ground floor. Here the late Patricia Mulholland is pictured in the centre of the front row, around 1925. (See also p. 16.)

Children from St Kevin's Primary School pose in the grounds of Clifton House. The buildings of Clifton Street are in the background.

Belfast Mercantile College, Glenravel Street, built by Mr James Pyper, was opened in 1874. It was later renamed Belfast High School and subsequently moved to Jordanstown.

Belfast Royal Academy was founded in 1785 in Donegall Street. In 1880 a new school on the Cliftonville Road, designed by Young & Mackenzie, was opened.

The Governors and staff of the Belfast Royal Academy stand on the front steps in 1927. Included are Mrs H.G. Woodward, Professor R.M. Henry (Queen's University, Belfast), A.R. Foster (headmaster), Mrs Anna Picken, Miss M. Hyndman, Miss A.I. Dickson, Mme Héritier-Ballantine, J.N. Shearman, C.C. Harte and G.B. Taylor.

Belfast Royal Academy's First XV in 1943/44 had Jack Kyle as captain. He later played for Ulster and Ireland and became a Fellow of the Royal College of Surgeons.

Seven
Churches

St James' Church of Ireland was built in 1869. All but the church tower and spire were destroyed in the air raids of 1941. It was rebuilt of natural stone and reconsecrated in 1954. The fourteenth-century bell was a gift from St Patrick's Cathedral in Dublin.

Members of the Band of Hope of St Anne's parish church are dressed in their best clothes for an outing, c. 1890.

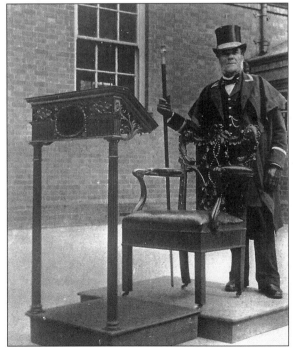

The Sovereign's Chair was originally in the old parish church for the use of the Sovereign (Mayor) of Belfast, attended by a Sergeant-of-Mace from the Town Hall.

The parish church of St Anne was built by Lord Donegall in 1776. The present cathedral was built around it while services were still being held. The old church was demolished in 1900 to allow the cathedral interior to be finished.

These are the choristers of St Anne's parish church in 1861. Standing second from the left is W.S. Baird, founder of the *Belfast Telegraph*. 'Amen' Browne is one of the gentlemen seated at the front.

St Joseph's church is situated near the Prince's Dock, where men are here seen riding on a timber raft, *c.* 1886.

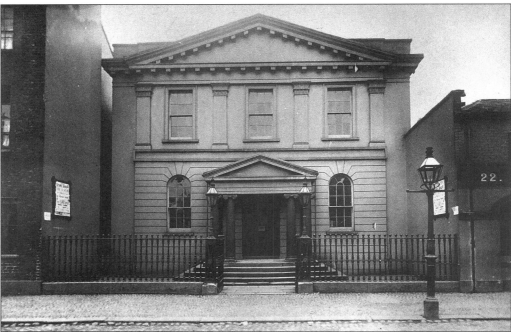

Frederick Street Methodist church was built in 1837. Along with several nearby churches it became part of the North Belfast Mission in 1898.

Duncairn Presbyterian church was opened in 1862. It was the first Presbyterian church in Belfast to have a bell hung in a tower. The original Lecture Hall can be seen in the background and Peeble Cottage is in the foreground.

Old St Patrick's church, Donegall Street, was consecrated in 1815. In his consecration discourse the Revd William Crolly acknowledged the monetary contribution made by the Protestants of Belfast. The congregation outgrew the building and it was replaced after 1876.

Sinclair Seamen's Presbyterian church in Corporation Street is famous for the many artefacts connected with the sea used in the church, for example the ship's wheel and bell.

St Paul's church, York Road, was built some 150 years ago in the prevailing style. The first Rector was Revd Mr Allen, followed by Revd Charles Scott.

Parishioners of St Mark's, Ballysillan, celebrate Empire Day on 24 May 1909 with a display of elaborate costumes.

All that was left of the vicarage of St Anne's parish church in 1968 is to the right of the cathedral. The railing and tree are thought to date from the early nineteenth century.

St Therese's church, Lisbreen, nears completion in Somerton Road in 1937.

The church of the Resurrection, Cavehill Road, was opened on Easter Sunday 1980. The foundation stone had been blessed by the Pope during his visit to Ireland in 1979.

Fortwilliam Park Presbyterian church was opened in 1885. The first minister was Revd Dr McConaghie. The building has an atelier – an unusual feature in a church.

The choir of St Peter's church, Antrim Road, *c.* 1954. Chancellor Breen and the choirmaster, Lister Wood, are seated in the front row.

The choir of Ekenhead Presbyterian church at the laying of the foundation stone of Ekenhead Memorial Halls, 20 October 1928.

Rosemary Presbyterian church in 1956. The church was formed by an amalgamation of the congregations of Ekenhead and Third Rosemary Street churches (the latter was destroyed by air raids in 1941).

Eight

Houses

Garden Hill (Gardenmore) House stood on what was to become North Queen Street. It was the home of Isaac Thompson, storekeeper of the Customs, and overlooked the Point Fields which ran down to the lough shore.

This was the courtyard of the Lyons family home in Oldpark Village and was built around 1750. The servants of the household occupied the houses.

Vicinage House and farm were advertised in the *Belfast Newsletter* in 1813 as being situated within half a mile of the Poor House (Clifton Street). In 1833 it became a seminary and later St Malachy's College.

Jennymount was built in around 1785 by Robert Thompson. The battlemented house was surrounded by many acres of parkland. It was renamed 'Castleton' in 1847 by the grandson of the builder, also called Robert.

The Grove was owned in 1807 by James Carson but changed hands several times until it was demolished after its last use as the District Headquarters of the Ulster Special Constabulary in 1926. The demesne extended from the shore of Belfast Lough to the Antrim Road.

Valentine Whitla, owner of Ben Eden in 1831, fenced off the grounds but provided a stile so that the right of way over the Cave Hill was not closed. It became home for the Redemptorist community in 1949.

Thronemount House on the Antrim Road was an attractive Georgian-style house. It became the Belfast Bible College and was later demolished.

Fortwilliam House was bought in 1809 by George Langtry, a general merchant and ship owner. He was the first man to have a steam vessel using the port of Belfast. Edward Langtry, his grandson, married Emile de Breton, the famous 'Jersey Lily'.

Mount Collyer was the residence of Dr James Drummond, the minister of Second Rosemary Street Unitarian church, in the early 1830s. He also conducted a boarding school for boys here.

The Lodge, Cliftonville Road, was a 'finishing school for young ladies'. There they learned how to conduct a tea party correctly, how to write letters and choose the proper dress for all occasions. The building later became a convent for the Poor Clares Order.

These were the last two thatched houses in Frederick Street and were taken down in the 1920s.

A typical Victorian house in Fortwilliam Park with the ubiquitous tower room. It now belongs to the Fold Housing Association.

Wingfield, a Regency-style house on the Cliftonville Road, was bought for £1,500 by Belfast Royal Academy in 1926 for use as a preparatory school. A swimming pool was constructed on the site some fifty years later.

These 'prefab' houses on the Shore Road were built immediately after the Second World War as temporary housing. Some lasted into the 1960s.

This Parish House at Greencastle no longer exists. Our Lady's Acre can be seen on the right.

This 400-year-old cottage in Sunningdale Park, the last building of its kind in Belfast, suffered an inglorious end. Following the collapse of the roof in continuous heavy rain, the cottage was demolished in 1987.

These cottages at Daddystown, Upper Cavehill Road, were built as quarry workers' dwellings in the early 1820s. Peggy Blair, who lived there until 1942, remembers her mother permitting 'Blitz evacuees' to sleep on the floor.

85

This late Victorian house in Waterloo Gardens is typical of those in the area. Note Mrs Kelly's musquash fur coat, fashionable in the late 1920s.

Somerton House once housed the preparatory department of Belfast High School. It subsequently became the first Northern Ireland Hospice.

This terrace of three Regency-style houses was built by Thomas Jackson in around 1831. Some seventy years later it became the Home for the Blind. When they moved out around 1980, the building was converted into flats by the Hearth Housing Association.

The wall plaque on this house in Brookhill Avenue identifies it as the childhood home of Louis McNiece, the famous poet.

These houses in Seaview Drive are typical of those built by Belfast Corporation in the inter-war years.

The Mount Vernon flats show the style of public housing popular with builders of the 1960s. The Northern Ireland Housing Executive is now responsible for all public housing.

Nine

Trade and Commerce

Henry Stewart had a grocery and butchery shop in Alexandra Park Avenue. His two sons, Wilson and Billy, are seated on the delivery cart pulled by Paddy the horse in 1924.

Mrs Ferris and daughter Bea stand at the door of her household goods shop on the Crumlin Road, c. 1916.

James Watson and an American visitor stand on the corner of Copperfield Street in front of Faulkner's grocery shop with a patrolling Royal Marine, 1970.

McCusker's Tea, Wine and Italian Warehouse was in Halliday's Road. The poster-covered building was demolished in 1915 to be replaced by the Lyceum Picture House the next year. A bottle of Fine Old Dublin whiskey could be bought for 21s.

The Old House in Little Patrick Street, seen here in around 1910, had a stabling yard and grain store. David Dalton, seen here with his wife and an employee, also sold wine and spirits.

Fleming's butchers shop was on the Antrim Road opposite the Waterworks. Note the extensive supply of meat and poultry for sale.

A baker's delivery boy watches the traffic in front of O.D. Cars' filling station, c. 1930. The clock in the shape of a giant petrol pump was a landmark for years on the Antrim Road.

Mrs Catherine Kelly, wife of the owner, poses in front of the shop of A. Kelly, House Furnisher, in Alexandra Park Avenue, early this century.

The Misses Johnston ran a dressmaking and millinery supply store at the corner of Willowbank Gardens. Margaret Johnston is seen here with her wares in around 1902.

McCune Brothers, on the Shore Road, sold hardware and delph, as now, but also had a fleshers and grocery shop. Note the boy's Eton collar.

This horse-drawn van of 1930, belonging to the Eglington Bakery, was unusual in having pneumatic tyres.

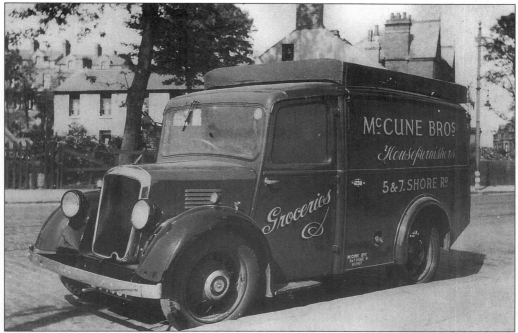

McCune Bros' 1936 Morris 10cwt van delivered not only groceries but also household goods.

Kirkwoods, who lived in this house on the Ballysillan Road, sold confectionery and tobacco products from their small attached shop.

The Duke of York Bar, on the left hand side of Commercial Court, has crates of bottles ready for delivery, 1968.

Fitzgerald, poulterer and fruiterer, had his shop on the Antrim Road beside Clifton Street Graveyard. This view dates from around 1904 – it is Christmas time, as the post office next door has Christmas cards for sale.

Number 12 Great Georges Street has had a chequered history. In 1837 it was occupied by James McNamara JP. By 1850 William Gelston had a provisioning and tobacco shop in it and in 1877 it was an RIC barracks. It is here seen re-erected in the Ulster Folk and Transport Museum.

The festive season is celebrated in the Phoenix Bar Antrim Road in 1947. The barman is James Lavery.

Samuel and Hugh Watt, sons of the owner, stand at the door of the saddler's and harness maker's shop in Agnes Street, *c.* 1922.

This family butchers, William Henderson and Sons, complete with sawdust, was on the Cliftonville Road in 1932 when this picture was taken. The beauty parlour upstairs had Water and Marcelle waving available to clients.

The Ulster Bank on Antrim Road in 1957 – it shows little change today. Note the gas lamps on the trolleybus standards and the Belisha beacons.

A cheerful Jimmy Moore displays the varied stock in his corner shop in Great Patrick Street in 1987.

Ten
People and Events

The marriage of John Walker and Mabel Johnston took place on 20 July 1904. Berta Johnston, William Johnston, Thomas Walker and Margaret Johnston were in attendance.

Francis Joseph Bigger was born on 17 July 1863 and was admitted a solicitor in 1887. He had many interests including archaeology and antiquities and was a member of the Royal Irish Academy. He supported the Irish language revival. He was the first Honorary Secretary of St Peter's parish church in 1896.

Ard Righ was F.J. Bigger's home for many years but has now been demolished.

Two sailors (former pupils) tell the children of Hemsworth Square School of their experiences in the 'Yang-tze Incident' in November 1949.

A clergyman and helpers make up Christmas gifts for the needy at North Belfast Mission in 1968.

The Duke of Abercorn is greeted at Belfast Docks by the American forces, *c.* 1942.

The Harbour Commissioners' new tug *Duchess of Abercorn* is launched, 25 August 1936.

Stephen Rea was born at home on the Antrim Road on Hallowe'en morning. In his twenties he joined the Abbey Theatre, starting a successful acting career. He was nominated for an Oscar for his part in *The Crying Game*.

Newington Primary School pupils dressed for their annual concert.

A Corpus Christi procession passes along Herbert Street in 1974.

Gerald Haldane, wearing the collarette of LOL 1131, walks with his brethren. The following banner belongs to LOL 1197.

Colonel Sir Francis Evans, who served with the Royal Ulster Rifles, was a pupil of Belfast Royal Academy. He served with distinction in the Diplomatic Corps as Ambassador to Israel and Argentina.

Kate Hoey, MP for Vauxhall and an old girl of the Belfast Royal Academy, presented the prizes in October 1993. Here she is accompanied by the Warden, C.F. Kennedy, the Headmaster, W. Sillery, the Head Girl, Suzanne Carroll, and the Head Boy, Andrew Adair.

Fortwilliam Park Presbyterian Church

Will be Opened for Public Worship

On SABBATH, the 26th April, 1885,

BY THE

REV. ROBERT FLINT, D.D., LL.D.,

Regius Professor of Divinity in the University of Edinburgh, and one of Her Majesty's Chaplains in Scotland.

Morning Service at 11-30.
Evening Service at 7-0.

The Committee respectfully request the favor of your attendance, with any of your family or friends.

A Collection will be taken up at each Service to meet the heavy balance due upon the building.

WM. JOHNSTON,

The invitation card to the opening of Fortwilliam Park Presbyterian church, 26 April 1885.

The Revd Dr McConaghie, the first minister of the church, had a daughter, Bessie, who became a Stormont MP.

Vivienne Scott MBE, formerly a missionary in India during the Second World War, worked in the Mariners' Mission in York Street. She raised thousands of pounds for the Cathedral Building Fund by collecting paper, rags and anything that would make money. She died on Christmas morning 1996, aged ninety-three.

John Cole, who lived at Skegoneill Avenue and was a pupil at the Belfast Royal Academy, became a well-known journalist and Political Editor with the BBC.

In the early part of the century children in need of healthcare were educated at Graymount Hospital Outdoor School.

Pupils of St Kevin's Boys' School celebrate their First Communion. Father O'Neill, Mrs Kerlin and Brother Byrne stand on the top step.

The Redemptionist Community of St Gerard's, 1989. Included are Revd Frank Toner, Revd Charles McNiffe, Revd Richard McMahon, Revd Robert Quinn, Brother Xavier and Brother Kieran.

Florence Lewis displays her party dress in 1920.

HMS *Sheffield* arrives in Dufferin Dock on Friday 1 June 1951, with HM Queen Elizabeth (now the Queen mother) and HRH Princess Margaret on board. They came to visit the Festival of Britain Exhibition at Castlereagh. In the small boat are Paddy McGreevy and Jimmy Knocker, employees of O'Prey Brothers, Belfast's oldest firm of boatmen.

James Galway, born in Carnalea Street, received his early flute training with the thirty-ninth Old Boys' Flute Band.

Currie Girls' Primary School on stage at the Assembly Hall of Church House, c. 1940. Included are Peggy Blair, Gloria Rosborough, Phyllis Dowie, Kathleen Davison and Grace Beasant.

The ladies of the Victoria Co-operative Guild celebrate at their annual dinner in the Midland Hotel. Molly Watson and her daughter Connie are on the left.

The ladies of Fortwilliam Golf Club hold their annual dinner on Lady Captain's Day in a Nissen hut which was situated in the present car park behind the eighteenth green.

Sir John Betjeman visited the cathedral
in 1975. Here he tells the Dean that St
Anne's is 'the finest modern cathedral'.

Dean Samuel Crooks, 'Black Santa',
began the Dean's Christmas Sit-Outs
for charity in the troubled years of the
Seventies.

Elizabeth has a drink in around 1955 in Glenbank Park, which was opened on 18 August 1923.

Ellen Dickson wanted someone to teach her how to 'flap her arms and legs together' so that she could swim. The Lord Mayor's Dream Machine arranged for Duncan Goodhew to do just that at the Grove Baths.

Members of Ekenhead Band of Hope take part in a pageant organized by the Irish Temperance League in 1937.

Three sets of twins join some sixty mothers and babies at the annual tea party at Mervue Street Baby Club in 1937.

William Russel Patey spent his first five years on board a tea clipper of which his father was master. He was commissioned in the Royal Irish Rifles in 1916. He was later attached to the Royal Flying Corps and was one of the first to win the DFC for gallantry and skill on bombing raids and photographic reconnaissance.

Sir Charles Russell, who died in 1900, was a pupil of St Malachy's College. He became MP for Dundalk and Attorney General in the Gladstone government of 1886-1892. He was a skilful advocate and exposed as forgeries the letters implicating C.S. Parnell in the Phoenix Park murders. As Lord Russell of Killowen, he was Lord Chief Justice of England and Wales.

Mr S.H. Hurwitz, at a dinner of the
Association of Jewish Ex-Servicemen,
welcomes Sir Francis Evans, seated on
his left, and Sir Basil Brooke on his
right.

Sir Otto Jaffe, born in Hamburg in
1846, came to Belfast with his family
where they set up a linen business. He
helped to establish the new synagogue
in Annesley Street and became Lord
Mayor of Belfast in 1899 and again in
1904. His name is remembered in the
Jaffe School which he built on the
Cliftonville Road, now demolished.

The children of class P1 in Ligoniel Primary School display their gifts for the elderly at the Harvest Service in 1972. Paul Ferguson, Colin Boreland and Heather Luney of P7 look after the little ones. Included are Rory Kennedy, Pamela McRoberts, Kim Bowers, Marina Graham, Jason Bates, Andrea Dickson, Jennifer Gordon and Rosemary Lyttle.

The workers in Gallaher Export Department (pipe tobacco) have decorated their workplace for the Coronation of King George VI.

Helen Waddell, scholar, dramatist and novelist, lived with her family in Cedar Avenue for some twenty years. Her best known novel is *Peter Abelard*.

Glynis Kirkwood and fellow pupils of the Girls' Model School chat to the Brazilian Ambassador in 1978 at a Council Education World Citizenship meeting.

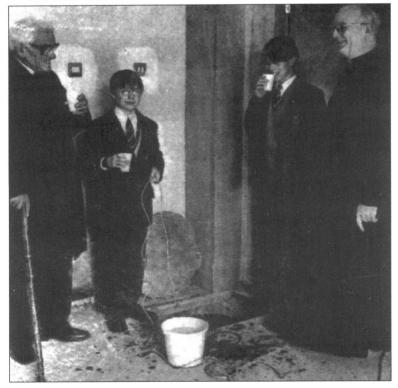

This old well was rediscovered when renovations were being made to St Malachy's College. It is 20ft deep and dates from the eighteenth century; it was originally beside a house called Vicinage.

This Chamberlain tramcar ran away, driverless, from the Cliftonville Road terminus and careered into a small shoemaker's shop beside the Phoenix Bar on the Antrim Road on 12 February 1946. Surprisingly no one was injured.

Albert McClure and May Thompson were married in Jennymount Methodist church on 8 July 1938. The Boys' Brigade and the Girls' Life Brigade form a guard of honour. (See also p. 18.)

A wartime wedding (*c.* 1941) with the bridegroom and best man in Royal Artillery uniform and the bride and bridesmaid in suits for which clothing coupons were required.

St Patrick's church, Donegall
Street, was the venue for this 1952
wedding. Pictured are Sean Falloon,
Sheila Miller, Edward O'Hara and
Bridie McErlean.

Connie Watson married Albert Duncan in Carlisle Memorial Methodist church, *c.* 1950.

Kathleen and Arthur pose at the foot of the winding staircase of Belfast Castle at their wedding in 1952.

The family group at the wedding of Patrick O'Hara and Maureen McKeever, in the Convent grounds, Crumlin Road.

The bride, Eveline Weir, was supported by her sister Margaret and sister-in-law Elizabeth at her marriage to Samuel Halliday, *c*. 1928. William Weir and Frank Morton were the groom's men.

Observe the changes in bridal styles in the wedding photographs contained in this section.

Acknowledgements

The North Belfast Historical Society is very grateful to all those who have helped in compiling this volume. Without the help and contributions from members and friends this venture would have been impossible.

Margaret Cartwright and Daphne McClements have made a huge contribution in time and effort and Kathleen Davison was responsible for all the word processing. Much help with copying and reprinting old photographs was given by Cyril Cartwright, Will McCrum, Adrian Mallon, Paddy Megahey, Harry O'Prey and Frank Rainey. Members of the Society who have contributed include: Robert Carson, Geraldine Birch, Ethel Hamilton, Fred Heatley, Jim and Pat Jenkins, L. Mann, Helen Moth, Brenda Nicholl, Olive Shaw, Patsy Rainey, Margaret Stuart, Esther Walker and Florence Whiteside.

Several friends of the Society and residents of North Belfast have contributed. These include Mrs G. Abernethy, George Allen, Elizabeth Anderson, Connie Buckley, Roy Brook, H.C. Casserley, John Coulter, Helen Diskin, Mr and Mrs R.J. Frame, Richard Graham, the Misses Henry, Mrs H. Kirkwood, Mr and Mrs Reg Maxwell, Elizabeth Madill, Tony Merrick, Christopher Neill, the McCune brothers, S. McAteer, Bernard McCloskey, Dan McGrady, Pearse McGrath, Jim McAllister, the O'Hara family, Veronica O'Prey, J.M. Penderleith, Michael Purdy, Mrs Rea, Mrs Tracey, Revd Frank Toner, W. Waid and R.J.S. Wiseman.

The Society is particularly grateful to the following institutions and organizations for giving us kind permission to reproduce their material: Belfast Bible College, Belfast Harbour Commissioners (R. Yeats), BBC Northern Ireland, Belfast High School (S. Littlewood), Belfast Royal Academy (E. McCamley), Cavehill Primary School, Department of the Environment for Northern Ireland, Environment and Heritage Service, Fortwilliam Golf Club, Holy Family Parish, Imperial War Museum London, War Memorial Heritage Centre Belfast, Linenhall Library (John Gray), North Belfast Scouts' Association (Derek Neill), Deputy Keeper of the Records, Public Record Office of Northern Ireland, Rosemary Presbyterian church (T.R. McMillen), The Dean of St Anne's Cathedral, St Malachy's College (G. McNamee), Seaview Primary School and the Ulster Architectural Heritage Society.

The Ulster Museum photographs on pages 2, 25, 32, 45, 53, 75 and 79 and the Ulster Folk and Transport Museum photographs on pages 10, 11, 23, 25, 29, 33, 35, 71, 81, 105 and 123 are reproduced by kind permission of the Trustees of the National Museum and Galleries of Northern Ireland.